IMAGES OF WAR

HITLER'S BOY SOLDIERS

RARE PHOTOGRAPHS FROM WARTIME ARCHIVES

Hans Seidler

D1709306

Edited by Charles Markuss

Pen & Sword
MILITARY

First published in Great Britain in 2013 by
PEN & SWORD MILITARY
An imprint of
Pen & Sword Books Ltd
47 Church Street
Barnsley
South Yorkshire
S70 2AS

Copyright © Hans Seidler, 2013

ISBN 978-1-84884-112-3

The right of Hans Seidler to be identified as author of this work has been asserted by him in accordance with the Copyright, Designs and Patents Act 1988.

A CIP catalogue record for this book is available from the British Library.

All rights reserved. No part of this book may be reproduced or transmitted in any form or by any means, electronic or mechanical including photocopying, recording or by any information storage and retrieval system, without permission from the Publisher in writing.

Typeset by Concept, Huddersfield, West Yorkshire
Printed and bound in England by CPI Group (UK) Ltd, Croydon, CR0 4YY.

Pen & Sword Books Ltd incorporates the Imprints of Pen & Sword Aviation,
Pen & Sword Family History, Pen & Sword Maritime, Pen & Sword Military, Pen & Sword Discovery,
Wharncliffe Local History, Wharncliffe True Crime, Wharncliffe Transport, Pen & Sword Select,
Pen & Sword Military Classics, Leo Cooper, The Praetorian Press, Remember When,
Seaforth Publishing and Frontline Publishing.

For a complete list of Pen & Sword titles please contact
PEN & SWORD BOOKS LIMITED
47 Church Street, Barnsley, South Yorkshire, S70 2AS, England
E-mail: enquiries@pen-and-sword.co.uk
Website: www.pen-and-sword.co.uk

Contents

Two young *Hitlerjugend* cadets observe with interest a *Luftwaffe* FlaK crew displaying their weaponry during a training exercise. In early 1943 the German youth were mobilized into special *Luftwaffe* auxiliary helpers. This was done in order to release many thousands of *Luftwaffe* FlaK men that were desperately required on the front lines. During 1943 some 11,500 *Hitlerjugend* boys were drafted as FlaK helpers. By the following year in 1944, some 55,000 were FlaK helpers, and by the end of the war over 200,000 FlaK helpers were known to be active on all fronts.

Introduction

From their beginnings in 1922 this book describes the history of the Hitler Youth or *Hitlerjugend*. This paramilitary organization of the Nazi Party was the second oldest Nazi group, and was made up of male youths aged fourteen to eighteen. By December 1936, the *Hitlerjugend* membership stood at just over 5 million. Each member was trained and natured towards Nazi ideology and the art of warfare.

With a host of rare and unpublished photographs with detailed captions this book shows how the *Hitlerjugend* evolved during the Second World War from an organization assisting in such organizations as the Reich Postal Service, *Deutsche Reichsbahn* (German State Railways), fire services, and Reich radio service, and served among anti-aircraft defence crews, to one of the most effective fighting formations in military history. The book describes how the *Hitlerjugend* were recruited into the elite *12.SS-Panzer-Division Hitlerjugend*, and traces how this *Waffen-SS* force fought on the battlefields of France, Hungary and the Eastern Front. Given sweets instead of cigarettes in their ration packs, it traces how various other *Hitlerjugend* formations fought to the death. Even when in full retreat before the Russians and Western Allies, it describes in detail how Hitler called upon the elderly veterans of the First World War to take up and defend their country alongside the *Hitlerjugend*. In front of overwhelming opposition Hitler's youth were ordered to delay the advance of the enemy and fight to the grim death. Although by May 1945, with the war over, various *Hitlerjugend* units, mostly dressed in civilian clothes, took to the hills and mountains of Bavaria and Austria and fought guerilla warfare. But as it had been during the war, these *Hitlerjugend* formations were neither well equipped or had the numbers of well trained soldiers to change the course of action through their defence.

Chapter One

Training and Preparation for War

Adolf Hitler was obsessed with youth as a political force, and the creation of the Hitler Youth or *Hitlerjugend* enabled him to meet this goal. He was able to use this uniformed army of teenagers not only for promoting the myth of his own 'invincible genius' but also in war. The *Hitlerjugend* had been for a number of years trained in diverse para-military skills. The most elite formations were the boys who served in the special units of the *Hitlerjugend*. In the *Flieger-HJ* or air training *Hitlerjugend*, there were more than 78,000 boys alone that had joined during the 1930s. Wearing their distinctive *Luftwaffe* blue uniforms with light blue piping and the armlet of the *Hitlerjugend*, they were trained in almost all aspects of aviation. Most members, between the ages of fourteen and eighteen in the *Flieger-HJ*, tried to obtain his 'wings': the A, B and C certificates in gliding.

Another special formation of the *Hitlerjugend* was the *Motorized-HJ*. Nearly every teenager from the age of sixteen onwards obtained his first driving licence for a motor cycle. But driving was only one part of the training. Not only did they learn a sound knowledge of both German and international traffic codes, but they also expertly trained in motor mechanics. The ultimate purpose of this training was self evident, as it would later serve in the motorized units of the *Wehrmacht*.

In northern Germany, it was very popular for the *Hitlerjugend* to join the *Marine-HJ*, the naval *Hitlerjugend*, which reached a total membership of nearly 62,000 boys. As in the case of other special formations of the *Hitlerjugend*, the *Marine-HJ* also demanded great mental and physical accomplishment. Before the war, all the necessary sailing certificates could be obtained, and each member had the opportunity to sail on vessels used by the German Navy for the training of its naval cadets.

Apart from the main formations of the *Hitlerjugend*, there were also a number of smaller components, including a signalling unit which did not commence until during the war. Another group formed was the *Reiter-HJ*, a cavalry unit which attracted mainly boys in rural areas.

When war broke out in 1939, a special unit of teenagers was created to be *Hitlerjugend* air-raid wardens. During these first months of war, about 1,091,000

Hitlerjugend were deployed for the war effort. Most of them were given meaningful tasks to help the German war economy. They were asked to collect from house to house scrap metal, copper, brass, razor blades, paper and bottles. And while one group collected, another stood in the background and sang German folk songs.

While the majority of the *Hitlerjugend* participated in the collection drive towards strengthening Germany's war machine, other parts, notably the para-military wing of the movement, were in full training. By the time Poland was defeated at the end of September 1939, vigorous military training was intensified. The intensification of their training was to gear Hitler's youth movement for fighting on the battlefield. Initially, those being recruited were expected to meet very stringent criteria. Every volunteer had to be fit with excellent racial features and produce a certificate of good behaviour from the Police. During their training programme new recruits were indoctrinated into an almost fanatical determination to obey the *Führer*, even if it meant shedding one's own blood on the battlefield. Though many did not know it, Hitler was already planning to create a military force out of the Youth.

Out on the battlefield the war had not gone to plan and many thousands of soldiers had perished as a consequence. The failure to capture Moscow in late December 1941 had been a complete disaster for the Germans on the Eastern Front. Germany's forces had altered out of recognition from its victorious summer operations. Due to the considerable recuperative powers of the *Heer*, in June 1942 another German summer offensive was launched. However, instead of attacking Moscow again Hitler ordered Army Group Centre to consolidate its positions whilst Army Group South advanced to the Caucasus and the Volga. The outcome of this grand manoeuvre saw the loss of Stalingrad and German forces being pushed back westward.

By July 1943 when the Germans unleashed their long awaited summer offensive codenamed 'Operation Zitadelle', the war in the East changed forever. Within two weeks of the attack, the offensive was abandoned, primarily due to a shortage of infantry replacements, the Allied invasion of Sicily and the heroic but costly Soviet defence. With stalemate on the Eastern Front, in the West the Allied bombing campaign over Germany intensified. In late 1943 Hitler began suspecting that there would soon be an Allied invasion of France and this would plunge Germany tactically into fighting a three-front war. With manpower at its lowest ebb Hitler was deter-mined more than ever to try to relieve the problem by turning to his youth move-ment. In his eyes they had been prepared for war with extensive military training. Now he was determined not only to see them fight on the battlefield, but to see them serve in an elite *Waffen-SS* formation. This would be alluring for the young recruits. By fighting in the realms of the *SS* order they would not only follow his orders to the letter but would not be afraid to shed their blood on the battlefield.

With the aid of scissor binoculars a *Heer* soldier points out to a group of children the great Fatherland in 1938. During the 1930s the Nazis ruthlessly indoctrinated children into the ideals of a new, greater German Reich. In Hitler's eyes the youth were vital to Adolf Hitler's purpose.

Inquisitive Sudeten children play around an eight-wheeled Sd.Kfz.263 *Panzerfunkwagon* armoured radio vehicle. The annexation of both Austria and Germany brought a huge wave of new members in the *Hitlerjugend* which, by the end of 1938, had reached a total membership of 8,700,000 children.

An Sd.Kfz.231 passes through a Sudeten village, with the streets littered with both young and old, cheering and yelling their support. Scenes such as this were common throughout the German-speaking part of Czechoslovakia. It was only weeks after the annexation that thousands of children would be enlisted into the *Hitlerjugend*.

Two photographs showing a group of Sudeten children giving a passing German vehicle their support and raising their right arms in salute. The children were soon to be absorbed into the *Bund Deutscher Mädel* (League of German Girls) for domestication. According to Nazi ideology, girls were expected to grow up to be good housewives with large families. They were told to produce pure children for the Fatherland and to be strong and obedient mothers.

Sudeten locals including children watch an armoured column cross the border during the annexation. Within weeks of the annexation the German Propaganda Office offered all Sudeten children, boys and girls, the chance to obtain books – full of National Socialist propaganda. The Propaganda Office specifically targeted its literature at the young people of the other German-speaking countries in Europe.

In a Sudeten square locals including children rejoice as German vehicles enter the town. Even before the annexation the German Propaganda Office, responsible for *Hitlerjugend* periodicals, founded a book club with the specific objective of spreading the word of National Socialism to thousands of Austrian and Czech children.

New children of the Reich, Austrian children, get the chance to observe and feel a real German weapon of war: a 37mm PaK35/36 anti-tank gun. The Nazis were very keen for children to be interested in the military, and for this reason many of them were initially indoctrinated by letting them become interested in weapons of war.

Three very young Austrian children are seated inside a Horch cross-country vehicle. The young boy on the left is wearing a M1938 field cap, whilst the boy on the right is wearing an M1935 steel helmet. These children would one day be inducted into the *Hitlerjugend* and would have grown into the youth movement already accustomed to being surrounded by the military.

A group of children inside the same Horch cross-country vehicle. From the very beginning Hitler made it known that the future of the German nation depended on its youth. The whole of German youth, he said, was to be educated, outside the parental home and school, and was to be physically, intellectually and morally in the spirit of National Socialism for service to the nation and community.

Hitlerjugend march along a road during an elaborate and impressive ceremony. Hitler was obsessed with youth as a political force, and the creation of the Hitler Youth or *Hitlerjugend* enabled him to meet this goal. He was able to use this uniformed army of teenagers not only for promoting the myth of his own 'invincible genius' but also in war.

Hitlerjugend rest during one of the many marches they had to endure. While this photograph was more than likely taken three or four years before war in Europe broke out, much of the Hitler Youth training was in preparation for war. Hitler was totally aware that the youth movement were a key instrument in maintaining the Nazi grip on power.

Two photographs showing the *Hitlerjugend*, one a group shot of an unidentified unit prior to a summer camp, and the other taken during a *Hitlerjugend* rally before the war. When the boys were together it was more than just a meeting of youths to enjoy themselves, they had a particular purpose. *Hitlerjugend* commanders were able to indoctrinate and influence the youth whilst they were away from their parents and loved ones. During these weekends the boys shared tents or huts, slept in dormitories, ate the same food, and slowly built up a camaraderie that was a far cry from family circumstances. Over the camp weekends the children were slowly fed Nazi propaganda and learned about racial ideology and how to spot a Jew. In this way, the youths were trained in preparation for military service whilst at the same time progressively taught the 'perils' of Jewish contamination. *(Roger Bender)*

Six photographs of the *Hitlerjugend* taken during the 1930s marching and playing the drums. The military emphasis during these youth meetings was a very important integral part of the training of these young children. Their commanders placed particular emphasis on the dedication to the greater glory of the Fatherland and meetings were constantly infused with military values. The uniforms, the ranks, the drilling, marching and parades all had a purpose. They were told by their commanders that they were special and were superior beings of the Aryan Master Race. Everything they undertook always had a military slant. *(Roger Bender)*

A *Hitlerjugend* ceremony played a very important part in the rank and file of the youth movement. Their commanding officers purposely drilled the boys in many parades and ceremonies, which they believed would create patriotism and loyalty within the ranks. This type of breeding allowed the boys to channel their natural boyish aggression into feeling superior and hating those that they regarded as hostile to the Reich. *(Roger Bender)*

A group of *Hitlerjugend* march through a town with their flags. Physical stamina was very important in the ranks of the Hitler Youth and was an important part of the youth training. It not only created physical fitness but instilled the young into believing that only the healthiest and strongest were superior. Military types of marching and discipline were inculcated into every youth. Nazi propaganda used many of these youth marches for visual material in their news reels. By marching and waving their flags they were able to display a sense of belonging and camaraderie and gave the German nation a sense of belonging and superiority. *(Roger Bender)*

4/86

The flag of the *Hitlerjugend* (Escort).

A photograph showing members of the *Hitlerjugend* undertaking woodwork under the supervision of their trainer. This type of training ensured that every member had diverse skills and the ability to build or construct. This would be particularly beneficial on the battlefield constructing shelters and other forms of protection. *(Roger Bender)*

A photograph of a *Hitlerjugend* recruit of the *Flieger-HJ*. *(Roger Bender)*

A photograph showing two *Hitlerjugend* trainers. There were more than 78,000 boys alone that had joined during the 1930s. Wearing their distinctive *Luftwaffe* blue uniforms with light blue piping and the armlet of the *Hitlerjugend*, they were trained in almost all aspects of aviation. Most members between the ages of fourteen and eighteen in the *Flieger-HJ*, tried to obtain their 'wings': the A, B and C certificates in gliding.

(*Roger Bender*)

Two photographs showing the *Hitlerjugend* training in what was known as the *Marine-HJ*, the naval *Hitlerjugend*. In northern Germany, it was very popular for the *Hitlerjugend* to join the *Marine-HJ*, which reached a total membership of nearly 62,000 boys. As in the case of other special formations of the *Hitlerjugend*, the *Marine-HJ* demanded great mental and physical accomplishment. Before the war, all the necessary sailing certificates could be obtained, and each member had the opportunity to sail on vessels used by the German Navy for the training of its naval cadets. (*Roger Bender*)

A very young *Hitlerjugend* stands to attention in front of his trainers inside a barracks. *(Roger Bender)*

Hitlerjugend trainers observe a bolt action rifle on a wooden tripod during a *Hitlerjugend* training exercise in the late 1930s. During their training programme new recruits were indoctrinated into an almost fanatical determination to obey the *Führer*, even if it meant shedding one's own blood on the battlefield. Though many did not know it, Hitler was already planning to create a military force out of the Youth. (*Roger Bender*)

Hitlerjugend march with national flags. This picture is more than likely a propaganda photograph taken during a Nuremburg rally. At these rallies the *Hitlerjugend* gathered *en masse* to listen to the *Führer*'s speeches, where they swore loyalty and marched before him. (*Roger Bender/Military Advisor*)

A photograph of a young *Hitlerjugend* officer. For young boys of the Hitler Youth, life was a combination of excitement, energetic activity, discipline, physical exercise and care for their bodies, indoctrination, and most of all a dedication to the glory of the Fatherland. (*Roger Bender/Military Advisor*)

Pictured on the left is Artur Axmann, leader of the *Hitlerjugend* leaving a building following a meeting with *Hitlerjugend* and *Heer* officers and staff. *(Roger Bender/Military Advisor)*

A photograph of what was known in Germany as The League of German Girls (*Bund Deutscher Mädel* or BDM). This was the girls' movement of the *Hitlerjugend*. It was the only female youth organization in Nazi Germany. At the beginning of the war the role of the BDM changed slightly, unlike their male counterparts they were not fed into the German armed forces but played their part in the war effort by collecting donations of money, clothing or old newspapers for the Winter Relief and other Nazi charitable organizations. However, in the last days of the war, some BDM girls were employed for defensive measures with their fellow *Hitlerjugend* and joined the *Volkssturm*. During the battle of Berlin the BDM were found manning FlaK guns and arming themselves with *Panzerfäuste* against advancing Russian tanks. A number of these girls were fanatic and often tried to defend their crude defences until they were killed. *(Roger Bender/Military Advisor)*

Nationalsozialistische Deutsche Arbeiterpartei
Hitler-Jugend / Reichsjugendführung

Postanschrift:
Berlin NW 40, Kronprinzenufer 10
Telegrammanschrift:
Reichsjugendführung — Berlin
Fernsprech-Sammel-Nummer: Stadtverkehr 41 00 11
Fernverkehr 41 68 41
Postscheck-Konto: Berlin Nr. 11 061

Zentralorgan der Partei:
„Völkischer Beobachter"

Amtliches Organ der RJf.:
„Die HJ."

| Büro des Stabsführers |
| Bg. |

Zeichen und Datum
sind bei Antwort stets anzugeben

Ihr Zeichen:

Gegenstand:

Berlin NW 40, am   2. März 1939

Herrn

Anliegend gebe ich das übersandte Bild mit dem Namenszug des Stabsführers zurück.

Anlage

Heil Hitler!.
i.A.

(Grimm)
Obergefolgschaftsführer

Stabsführer der HJ.
LAUTERBACHER

A photograph and a *Hitlerjugend* identity paper of *Stabsführer* Hartmann Lauterbacher of the *Hitlerjugend* in March 1939. Between 1932 and 1933, Lauterbacher was appointed leader of the Westphalia Lower Rhine area, and between 1933 and 1934 he was appointed high area leader of the Hitler Youth West. On 22 May 1934, Baldur von Schirach appointed Lauterbacher his deputy and staff leader. In 1936, Lauterbacher functioned as a member of the *Reichstag*, as of April 1937 as a ministerial advisor. In 1940, Lauterbacher was appointed *Gauleiter* of the Gau of South Hanover Braunschweig. During the war he also found himself having to spend a few weeks training in an SS formation. (*Roger Bender/Military Advisor*)

Chapter Two

Recruitment into the
Waffen-SS

By the end of 1943, nearly every boy of sixteen and seventeen was undergoing pre-military training in camps. As the war dragged on, *Hitlerjugend* leaders and fanatical *SS* officers conspired to use these boys as frontline soldiers. In their eyes, it was a children's crusade to strengthen the crumbling defences and offer the thousands of teenagers a final sacrifice in the name of their beloved Führer. As Goebbels coined his famous propaganda slogan of 'Total War', a massive recruiting drive of the war *Waffen-SS* was made which heavily concentrated on the *Hitlerjugend*. So eager were they to get the boys into *SS* uniforms, there were even radio advertisements, recruiting placards, and posters distributed all over the country. Under the impact of propaganda, a special legendary division of the *Hitlerjugend* was created within the realms of the *Waffen-SS*, which ultimately became known as the *12.SS-Panzer-Division Hitlerjugend*. At first Goebbels objected to using the name as he was concerned that it might provide the Allies with propaganda. But Hitler did not agree, and on 16 February 1943, Himmler's *SS* commanders began their first talks about creating an *SS-Hitlerjugend*. Four months later, an *SS-Hitlerjugend* division was finally born.

Initially, it was agreed that the recruits were to be drawn from the *Hitlerjugend*, using teenagers aged about seventeen, but frequently sixteen-year-olds and even younger boys were drafted into the SS-Division. Here in the *Waffen-SS*, the *Hitlerjugend* would be put to the ultimate test. If it conducted itself well, it was proposed that other German divisions, especially the *Heer* elite division, *Grossdeutschland* would be the most suitable army division for integrating a large number of youths into its ranks. However, this idea was soon rejected and the *Hitlerjugend* volunteers, other than joining the *SS*, were drawn in sizable numbers into the *Volksgrenadier* divisions.

During July and August 1943, nearly 10,000 young conscripts arrived at the training camp Beverloo in Belgium, the majority of which were still only sixteen years old. Most of them had volunteered for other branches of the armed services, mainly the U-boat branch of the navy and the *Luftwaffe*. But after being subjected to various kinds of persuasion, moral blackmail, or simply being talked into volunteering for the SS, they soon found themselves in *Waffen-SS* barracks.

These youngsters represented a large cross-section of the German youth whose background had made them vulnerable to the ideas and beliefs of National Socialism. Many of them had already lost their fathers in the war. Their mothers were often working away from home, helping the war effort. A large majority had witnessed first hand the death and destruction of war, serving as young anti-aircraft helpers in the cities, feeling the full impact of the Allied bomber offensive. Evacuated or bombed out from their homes, the military offered them a kind of security. Some boys that entered the training camps were undernourished and many instructors reported that the boys were found to be physically weak on reporting for duty. Their condition was taken into account during the initial training set out by the *Hitlerjugend* Division for recruits.

In total, fifty officers had been drafted in as replacements to compensate for the terrible shortages of experienced officers and NCOs among the teenagers. Their first commander was a highly decorated thirty-four-year-old *SS-Brigadefuhrer* General Fritz Witt, who enjoyed a very high reputation among the soldiers of both the *Waffen-SS* and *Heer* units: in the *Hitlerjugend* great importance was placed upon a good formal relationship between the boys and their officers. Company commanders strove, where possible, to establish contact with the parents of their recruits. The commanders were constantly aware of the psychological burden between the boys and their parents, and great emphasis was put on morale. Discipline was therefore not harsh, and 'duty and order' to the division was maintained with some compromises. Out on exercise, however, there was no time for leniency. Training was gruelling and aggressive, routinely conducted for three days each week. Call-out 'Alarm' exercises and airborne training were undertaken during the night to avoid air-attack. They simulated as closely as possible real combat conditions using live ammunition. The lessons learned on the Eastern Front and the tactics used by the Russian infantry and armour were instilled in the minds of every boy. It was this high quality training and leadership that succeeded in overcoming the initial worries of their young recruits. For Witt it was a blessing, because he knew that one day these young fearless warriors would have to be put to the real test and spill blood on the battlefield.

Throughout the summer of 1943 the *SS-Hitlerjugend-Division* continued military training in Beverloo. Although there was a shortage of uniforms to go around, the psychological outlook among the boys was good. They had quickly generated a sense of belonging and unit pride. This would be an essential ingredient to any combat formation that was to have any staying power on the battlefield.

The organization of the *SS-Hitlerjugend-Division* comprised two infantry regiments, one panzer regiment, one engineer battalion, one artillery regiment, and a detachment each of reconnaissance, anti-aircraft, anti-tank, and signalling. In October 1943, the *SS-Hitlerjugend-Division* was renamed the *12.SS-Panzer-Division Hitlerjugend*. But the division lacked sufficient armour. To supplement this badly equipped force, four up-gunned Pz.Kpfw.IVs and four Panthers were officially pulled out from operations on the Eastern Front and sent West, much to the anger of the German Army command. The artillery regiment too had very few artillery pieces, and general transport consisting of lorries, cars, and traction vehicles hardly existed. In order to overcome this problem the division requisitioned a number of vehicles from the Italian Army, and where possible augmented their own German vehicles with other foreign vehicles. However, during late 1943 and the early months of 1944, the *12.SS-Panzer-Division Hitlerjugend* received new batches of equipment which radically transformed the division. By early spring 1944, the division's armour shifted to Hasselt in Belgium, enabling it to carry out actual divisional exercises as a fully fledged Panzer Division. Both Field-Marshal von Rundstedt, the Commander-in-Chief West, and Panzer pioneer and renowned commander, General Heinz Guderian, made a special visit to Hasselt to observe first hand the exercises of the division. Here they paid a warm tribute to the boys for their outstanding professionalism and high efficiency which they had achieved in rapid time.

By 1 June 1944, the *1st Panzer-Corps* announced that the *12.SS-Panzer-Division Hitlerjugend* was fully prepared for military operations. Although it still lacked the *Werfer* or rocket launcher, and *Panzerjäger* or anti-tank battalions, their commanders were confident of performing any task in the West. Well trained and proudly wearing their distinctive SS uniforms, these teenagers were formidable opponents. Issued with sweets in their ration packs instead of cigarettes, they were as deadly as their adult counterparts. With littler to lose, each boy was willing to fight an heroic battle in the name of the Führer, and even die for him on the battlefield.

A *Hitlerjugend* poster, which were distributed in their thousands all over the Reich during the 1930s and the early part of the war. The poster reads 'Youth serves the Führer' and 'all ten-year-olds to the HJ'. Hitler was obsessed with youth as a political force, and the creation of the *Hitlerjugend* enabled him to meet this goal. In recruiting these young people he was able to use this uniformed army of teenagers not only for promoting the myth of his own 'invincible genius' but also in war.

This is just one of the many *Waffen-SS* recruiting posters that were distributed throughout the *Reich* to urge youths to volunteer for the *SS-Hitlerjugend Division* in 1943. The poster reads 'You too'.

Waffen-SS 80mm mortar crew during operations on the Eastern Front probably in 1942. With manpower at its lowest ebb Hitler was determined more than ever to try to relieve the problem by turning to his youth movement. In his eyes they had been prepared for war with extensive military training. Now he was determined not only to see them fight on the battlefield, but to see them serve in an elite Waffen-SS formation. To Hitler the thought of these teenagers dressed in the special camouflaged SS uniforms would be alluring for the young recruits. By fighting in the realms of the SS order they would not only follow Hitler's order to the letter but would not be afraid to shed their blood on the battlefield. (HITM)

Two SS recruits with a MG34 machine gun on the sustained-fire mount. As the war dragged on, *Hitlerjugend* leaders and fanatical SS officers conspired to use these boys as frontline soldiers. In their eyes, it was a children's crusade to strengthen the crumbling defences and offer the thousands of teenagers a final sacrifice in the name of their beloved Führer. (HITM)

SS recruits with a MG34 machine gun on the sustained-fire mount. This weapon was regarded in 1943 as more than enough to keep open the flanks for attacking infantry. Many successful engagements were made by the SS using both the MG34 and MG42 machine gun. The MG42 especially had an awesome reputation as it had a cyclic firing rate of 1,200 (later 1,500) rounds per minute, or up to three times its Allied equivalents. *(HITM)*

A camouflaged vehicle during a training exercise. The organization of the *SS-Hitlerjugend-Division* comprised two infantry regiments, one panzer regiment, one engineer battalion, one artillery regiment, and a detachment each of reconnaissance, anti-aircraft, anti-tank, and signalling. In October 1943, the *SS-Hitlerjugend-Division* was transformed and renamed the 12.*SS-Panzer-Division Hitlerjugend*. But the division lacked sufficient armour.

A familiar sight showing a *Waffen-SS* regiment sweeping across a field during operations in the summer of 1943. The *Hitlerjugend* learned much from the techniques and skills of the *Waffen-SS* on the Eastern Front and during training exercises in Belgium during 1943 and early 1944 practising tactics on the battlefield.

A training exercise showing a *Hitlerjugend* crew using their 20mm FlaK 30 in a ground mounted role. A typical five man crew comprised the gun commander, layer (gunner), range setter, loader and rangefinder operator. In 1943 the *Hitlerjugend* had few FlaK, PaK or artillery pieces. Throughout the summer of 1943, the *SS-Hitlerjugend-Division* continued military training in Belgium. Although there was a shortage of uniforms to go around, the psychological outlook among the boys was good. They had quickly generated a sense of belonging and unit pride. This would be an essential ingredient to any combat formation that was to have any staying power on the battlefield. *(HITM)*

A *Hitlerjugend* 75mm PaK 40 crew during a training exercise in 1943. This training simulated as closely as possible real combat conditions using live ammunition. The lessons learned on the Eastern Front and the tactics used by the Russian infantry and armour were instilled in the minds of every youth. Training was gruelling and aggressive, but these recruits soon became excellent fearless warriors, which made them fighting elite. (*HITM*)

An *SS* soldier with an MG42 machine gun on the sustained-fire mount. The MG34 and MG42 were very effective general purpose machine guns and on their sustained mounts in an AA role were more than capable of damaging, or even bringing down, an aircraft. A well sighted, well hidden and well-supplied MG34 or MG42 could hold up an entire attacking regiment, and could inflict heavy losses on an enemy advance. (*HITM*)

During a parade ceremony the commander of the *Hitlerjugend*, Artur Axmann takes the salute. *(Roger Bender)*

During a parade commanders inspect a *Hitlerjugend* soldier. *(Roger Bender)*

A *Hitlerjugend* recruit poses for the camera dressed in his *Heer* greatcoat and field cap and displaying his *HJ* arm band. *(Roger Bender)*

Here an SS poster from 1943 recruits *Hitlerjugend* into the *12.SS-Panzer-Division*. The poster reads 'come to us'. Both *Hitlerjugend* leaders and fanatical SS officers conspired to use the youth as frontline soldiers. In their eyes it was a children's crusade to strengthen the crumbling defences and offer the thousands of teenagers a final sacrifice in the name of their beloved Führer.

SS-Reichsführer Heinrich Himmler commander of the SS feebly pats the cheek of a young child at a Nazi rally. In Himmler's eyes the youth were the inspiration of the Fatherland, and he was keen to use their para-military training on the battlefield. He was convinced that their indoctrination would stir-up fanatical hatred for their foe.

Chapter Three

The Baby-Division

In May 1944, the new *Hitlerjugend* division was transported by rail from Belgium and was moved close to its expected area of action between the lower Seine and Orne rivers.

The *Hitlerjugend* division was the nearest of all the four *Waffen-SS* divisions to the actual Allied landing point. On paper the division had over 20,000 soldiers deployed for action in Normandy. Although it was short of a number of armoured vehicles, the troops were well equipped and armed. After nine months of intensive combat training their spirits were high and they were looking at the coming action with confidence.

Just hours before the Allied landings began the *12.SS-Panzer-Division* headquarters were informed that enemy paratroopers had jumped behind the coastal sector in Normandy. This, it was predicted, was the prelude to the main attack. A couple of hours later all units of the *Hitlerjugend* were made ready and prepared in their alarm positions. Ninety minutes before the Allied landings began the *OKW* (*Oberkommando der Wehrmacht*) assigned the 12.SS to *Heeresgruppe B*. And yet, despite measures, assessments and orders of the German high and supreme command offices on the growing developments of an Allied landing, the *Hitlerjugend* were not released for action. Even when the enemy landed at 06:30 hrs, *OKW* still forbade them from being released, but did approve its advance.

During the course of 6 June convoys of trucks and Panzers of the division navigated the congested narrow roadways of Normandy, moving first into the area around Lisieux and then southwest of the city of Caen. During its march, in particular from early afternoon, the *Hitlerjugend* were constantly strafed by fighters, which disrupted the cohesion of many of the marching columns. By the following morning on 7 June, exhausted from more than a day's constant marching, the bulk of the *Hitlerjugend* had moved into the area north of Caen. By this time reports had confirmed that the enemy had managed to break through some parts of the coastal defences and pushed his attack inland. By 09.00 hrs *Sturmbannführer* Kurt Meyer, the commander of '*Panzer Meyer*', a *Kampfgruppe* (improvised battle-group) comprising three battalions of infantry and a considerable number of Pz.Kpfw.IV tanks, had set up his forward command post in the Ardennes abbey. An hour later the first Panzers of the division moved forward into their assembly areas followed by young *SS* grenadiers wearing their distinctive green, yellow and brown camouflage smocks. Hidden beneath straw and branches the Panzers trained their powerful 75mm gun barrels towards the advancing enemy. From their positions they could make out the stout, olive-green Sherman tanks moving slowly across the front of their *Kampfgruppe* towards the Caen-Bayeux road. Suddenly the Shermans opened fire and the first Panzer erupted in smoke and flame. Others were also hit and set ablaze by Canadian anti-tank guns. From their hideouts and freshly dug trenches, the youths crashed into action, opening up a ferocious barrage of fire on British and Canadian positions. At times the fighting was at close quarters, the boys pitching grenades and pumping machine-gun fire into the enemy lines. Although the continuous attack from the air disrupted the grenadier's assault, the teenagers of the *12.SS* fought on. In the nearby village of Malon, the boys were feverishly taking up positions, stalking the enemy tanks with their deadly *Panzerfaust* rocket launchers and destroying several of them. In total the grenadiers knocked out twenty-eight enemy tanks at a loss of six of their own. Many of the Allied soldiers were shocked at seeing teenagers in *SS* uniforms. It was their first encounter with the *Hitlerjugend* generation. For months prior to the invasion of Normandy, the Allies had ridiculed the *Hitlerjugend* as the 'baby-division'. But to the soldiers that fought against the *12.SS*, this was far from a division of badly trained teenagers. It was an elite division that inspired fear and, at the same time, fought a battle that even inspired its enemies.

Over the next few days, as the battle of Normandy intensified, the *Hitlerjugend* came under even heavier attacks. But still this did not discourage the grenadiers from being driven from their bombed and blasted positions, for they had been given orders to hold the enemy at all costs and prevent them from penetrating their lines and breaking through to the ancient city of Caen. During the evening of 9 June the *Panzer-Lehr-Division* moved into line alongside the *12.SS* after driving miles to the front from Chartres. The following day the *21.Panzer-Division* also moved up and helped the other two divisions form the principal shield around Caen, with a motley group of other ad hoc units that had retreated from the coastal sector. For the next days and weeks that followed the *Hitlerjugend*, '*Lehr*' division and the *21.Panzer-Division* carried on fighting superbly in and around the city of Caen, which was slowly being reduced to rubble. All day and night the fighting raged. Many soldiers were killed at point blank range, whilst others fighting in the hedgerows and ditches, fought to the death. Through the lanes and farm tracks that criss-crossed the Normandy country-side, rows of dead from both sides lay sprawled out amid a mass of hand grenades and smashed and burnt out vehicles.

On 14 June the commander of the *12.SS*, *Brigadeführer* Fritz Witt was killed at his divisional command post in Venoix, near Caen and was replaced by Kurt Meyer. At only 33 years old, with Iron Cross, First and Second Class and the Knights Cross with

Oak Leaves, Meyer was the youngest divisional commander in the German armed forces. Out on the battlefield he was a daredevil commander of unorthodox methods and fought his battles deep inside enemy lines. But despite his skill and courageous character the change of command in the 12.*SS* made no tactical difference. In fact, he took command of the division with it being on the edge of disaster. Fighting for the defence of Caen had continued with massive losses, despite the preparation of new defences to prevent an enemy offensive on the city.

By the morning of 26 June, the British finally unleashed a large-scale attack on Caen code-named '*Operation Epsom*'. During the days fighting at least fifty enemy tanks were knocked out by the Panzers and PaK guns alone. But the Panzergrenadiers took a heavy battering, and in some areas a number of battalions were totally wiped out along with their commanders. Over the next few days the Allies continued to strike out smashing onto the 12.*SS* lines and causing massive damage to their positions. In the days leading up to July, the British endeavouring to expand their bridgehead, became increasingly incensed at the conduct of the *Hitlerjugend* division, who fought so tenaciously when their cause was so clearly lost. This dogged determination had managed to finally blunt the 'Epsom' operation, which consequently prevented it from achieving the high plain south of Caen. But in spite of this success the division was badly depleted and its survivors exhausted. Most of the German forces around the city were in desperate need of being replenished.

On 5 July, news reached *Heeresgruppe B* that Hitler contemplated having the *Hitlerjugend* relieved. However, three days later the *SS* division were once again fighting another battle for Caen, codenamed by the Allies as '*Operation Charnwood*'. Once again Meyer's 'boys' were the core of the defence, and fought out the battle in the ruins around Caen with an aura that they were indestructible, even though their ranks had been decimated after weeks of continued defence. As the battle reached its peak, Hitler ordered the city to be held at all costs. But with no more reserves left and ammunition rapidly running out, Meyer ordered the withdrawal of the division and instructed them take on a new defensive position in the rear.

By 11 July the *Hitlerjugend* was relieved by the '*Leibstandarte Adolf Hitler*' division, which took command of two units that remained in action.

Fighting continued to be fierce in France and by the end of the first week of August both the *Heer* and *Waffen-SS* divisions were fighting for survival. Corps and divisions remained in action on paper, but were becoming a collection of small battles, shrinking down to battalion size. A catastrophe now threatened the whole area as the Americans began to break out and the Normandy campaign became mobile. To save the German forces in Normandy from being completely encircled and destroyed a series of rapid withdrawals were undertaken through the Falaise-Argentan gap. On 16 August German forces continued retreating and crossed the River Orne. The *Hitlerjugend* division desperately fought to keep the gap open. The bulk of the

German armour, however, that had become trapped inside the pocket at Falaise fought a desperate battle to escape the impending slaughter. By 21 August, the terrible fighting in what became famously known as the battle of the 'Falaise Pocket' drew to a catastrophic conclusion. The *Waffen-SS* had been dealt a heavy blow.

The Normandy campaign had been very costly for the *Waffen-SS*, with many of its elite units being annihilated. Those elements that managed to escape the slaughter were withdrawn and refitted.

With many of the elite *SS* units recuperating following the Normandy campaign Hitler wanted no respite and decided to launch a great winter counter-attack in the West. The attack he envisaged would be through the Ardennes – the scene of his great 1940 victory – and capture the town of Antwerp. 'Fog, night, and snow', would be on his side. With Antwerp in German hands, he predicted the British and Americans would have no port from which to escape, but this time the enemy would not be allowed to escape.

Here in the Ardennes a substantial number of divisions were assigned to the area, including four crack *Waffen-SS*; 1.SS.'*Leibstandarte Adolf Hitler*', 2.SS.'*Das Reich*', 9.SS.'*Hohenstaufen*', and 12.SS.'*Hitlerjugend*'. By mid-December, all German forces were in place and ready to unleash the largest offensive since Kursk two years before.

At first the Ardennes offensive went well for the 12.SS but within a week the Allies began to recover from the initial surprise and resistance stiffened day by day. By 22 December the Americans began stemming the German drive. Coupled with the lack of fuel and the constant congestions on the narrow roads many German units were brought to a standstill.

By 24 January all four *Waffen-SS* divisions that were initially committed to the Ardennes campaign were withdrawn and ordered to Hungary in a drastic attempt to throw the Red Army back across the Danube and to relieve the capital, Budapest. As for the remaining forces in the Ardennes sector they were withdrawn and the remaining units were back over the Rhine by 10 February, preparing to fight the last battle of the *Reich*.

A youthful soldier sits in the passenger seat of a Schwimmwagen amphibious vehicle during summer operations in 1944. In the distance stationary in a field is a reworked Panther Ausf.D belonging to 5th Company's Co and an Sd.Kfz.251 Ausf.D halftrack. (*HITM courtesy of Michael Cremin*)

Young SS on the battlefront wearing their camouflage smocks during late summer on the Eastern Front. These men played a decisive part in helping support and stiffen the front lines against the growing might of the Red Army. By 1944 a number of *Hitlerjugend* were employed to help replenish the losses sustained and assist in defending against enemy attacks.

A *Hitlerjugend* rare 30mm FlaK 103/38 gun being used against ground targets. This was a very powerful but unreliable weapon not available until the Summer of 1944. By 1 June 1944, the 1st *Panzer-Corps* announced that the 12.*SS-Panzer-Division Hitlerjugend* was fully prepared for military operations. Although it still lacked the Werfer or rocket launcher, and *Panzerjäger* or anti-tank battalions, their commanders were confident of performing any task in the West. Well trained and proudly wearing their distinctive *SS* uniforms, these teenagers were lethal opponents. Issued with sweets in their ration packs instead of cigarettes, they were as deadly as their adult counterparts. With littler to lose, each boy was willing to fight an heroic battle in the name of the Führer, and even die for him on the battlefield.

Hitlerjugend advance forward into action in the Caen area in June 1944. During the course of 6 June 1944 convoys of trucks and Panzers of the division navigated the congested narrow roadways of Normandy, moving first into the area around Lisieux and then southwest of the city of Caen. During its march, in particular from early afternoon, the *Hitlerjugend* were constantly strafed by fighters, which disrupted the cohesion of many of the marching columns. By the following morning on 7 June, exhausted from more than a day's constant marching, the bulk of the *Hitlerjugend* had moved into the area north of Caen. By this time reports had confirmed that the enemy had managed to break through some parts of the coastal defences and pushed his attack inland.

A *Hitlerjugend* soldier keeps watch in the Caen sector of Normandy. For months prior to the invasion of Normandy, the Allies had ridiculed the *Hitlerjugend* as the 'baby-division'. But to the soldiers that fought against the 12.*SS*, this was far from a division of badly trained teenagers. It was an elite division that inspired fear and, at the same time, fought a battle that even inspired its enemies. In front of Caen the boys of the *HJ* feverishly took up positions, stalking the enemy tanks with their deadly *Panzerfäuste*, and destroying several of them. Many of the Allied soldiers were shocked at seeing teenagers in *SS* uniforms. It was their first encounter with the *Hitlerjugend* generation.

Soldiers of the *12.SS-Panzer-Division* wade through a marsh in northern France. Over the next few days, as the battle of Normandy intensified, the *Hitlerjugend* came under even heavier attacks. But still this did not discourage the grenadiers from being driven from their bombed and blasted positions, for they had been given orders to hold the enemy at all costs and prevent them from penetrating their lines and breaking through to the ancient city of Caen.

A MG34 machine gun on a heavy mount in the Normandy sector in June 1944 more than likely covering an advancing rifle company. A typical infantry battalion's machine gun company had two heavy machine gun platoons, each with four guns. In open terrain they would protect the flanks of advancing rifle companies, as in this photograph.

Two *Hitlerjugend* troops keep low to avoid enemy fire during operations in June 1944. All day and night the fighting raged in northern France. Many soldiers were killed at point blank range, whilst others fighting in the hedgerows and ditches, fought to the death. Through the lanes and farm tracks that criss-crossed the Normandy countryside, rows of dead from both sides lay sprawled out amid a mass of hand grenades and smashed and burnt out vehicles.

(*Opposite*) A young *Hitlerjugend* soldier lays out a national flag more than likely for aerial recognition. The casual approach to concealment from the air suggests that this depicts a training exercise. To remain in the open during fighting in Normandy with such a conspicuous object was to invite certain death. During their defence of the Normandy sector the *HJ Panzergrenadiers* took a heavy battering, and in some areas a number of battalions were totally wiped out along with their commanders. Over the next few days the Allies continued to strike out smashing onto the 12.SS lines and causing massive damage to their positions. In the days leading up to July, the British endeavouring to expand their bridgehead, became increasingly incensed at the conduct of the *Hitlerjugend* division, who fought so tenaciously when their cause was so clearly lost. This dogged determination had managed to finally blunt a series of Allied attacks. But in spite of this success the division was badly depleted and its survivors exhausted. Most of the German forces in France were in desperate need of being replenished.

Hitlerjugend troops move forward into action. Despite its severe mauling by Allied bombing, the division was far from beaten and fought on courageously. All over the Normandy sector the *HJ* division continued desperately trying to contain the Allies in check. The Norman countryside had created conditions that favoured the *SS* grenadiers. Clusters of trees, tall hedges, ditches, and lack of roads frustrated the Allied armoured units seeking to destroy enemy tanks in open areas. Aided by this terrain the *SS* were able to defend positions longer than the Allies had considered possible, and as a result incurred huge casualties. Frequently the Allies watched their irrepressible foe come under a furious crescendo of mortar and shellfire, and still they held their ground to the grim death. However, the savage Allied air attacks and naval bombardments gradually began to grind down the German defences. Movement was almost impossible by daylight, and any vehicles that travelled during the day were attacked and destroyed.

HJ troops during operations against British forces in a field. By mid July 1944 both the *Heer* and *Waffen-SS* divisions were fighting for survival. Corps and divisions remained in action on paper, but were becoming a collection of small battle groups.

Soldiers of the *12.SS-Panzer-Division* take cover during extensive fighting in Normandy. The position here comprises a 75mm l.IG18 field gun placed overlooking open terrain. This particular weapon was used in direct infantry support. The gun was very versatile in combat and the crew often aggressively positioned it, which usually meant the piece was regularly exposed on the battlefield, as seen here. The careless concealment suggests that this is a training exercise.

An *SS* grenadier dismounts from his well-concealed Sd.Kf.251 Ausf.D halftrack. During the battle of Normandy the *Hitlerjugend* continued to fight on for days and weeks. For four weeks they battled without relief and as a consequence suffered huge losses in both men and equipment. By mid July 1944 the division had suffered 60 per cent casualties, a third of whom were killed.

A well concealed machine gunner watches some of his comrades returning after a reconnaissance patrol. The MG42 is mounted on a sustained fire mount. All the grenadiers can be seen armed with 9mm MP38/40 machine pistols, one of the most effective submachine guns ever produced. The MP38/40 machine pistol was commonly called the 'Schmeisser' although the gun designer, Hugo Schmeisser, had nothing to do with its design by the German weapons manufacturer Erma.

A well camouflaged Sd.Kfz.252 halftrack of the 12.SS passes a knocked out American halftrack during the division's withdrawal from the Normandy sector in July 1944. The halftrack has been covered with foliage in order to break up the distinctive shape of the vehicle. Travelling by day like this across the Normandy countryside was very dangerous and often German vehicles were attacked with great loss. (*HITM courtesy of Michael Cremin*)

Two photographs showing SS troops in action with their 50mm mortar against an enemy target. Each battalion fielded six of these excellent 80mm sGrW 34 mortars, which could fire fifteen bombs per minute to a range of 2,625 yards. Aside from high-explosives and smoke bombs, this weapon also fired a 'bounding' bomb. It was normally very common for infantry, especially during intensive long periods of action, to fire their mortar from either trenches or dug-in positions where the mortar crew could also be protected from enemy fire. Although this weapon was very effective during infantry fighting the mortar was not a very accurate weapon. Generally it required several projectiles to achieve a direct hit on a target. (*HITM courtesy of Michael Cremin*)

A photograph of a *Hitlerjugend* grenadier armed with an MG42 machine gun during operations in Normandy, probably in July 1944. Some soldiers were so young that in their rations they had sweets instead of tobacco. All of them were ordered to stand and fight and not to abandon their positions. These soldiers of the famous 'baby-division' were inspired by fear and hatred of their enemy, and as a result often fought to the death. *(IWM/M. Kaludow)*

Soldiers of the *Hitlerjugend* armed with the famous MG42 machine gun during a lull in the fighting in France in July 1944. By the end of the first week of August both the *Heer* and *Waffen-SS* divisions were fighting for survival. Corps and divisions remained in action on paper, but were becoming a small collection of battle groups, shrinking down to battalion size. A catastrophe now threatened the whole area as the Americans began to break out and the Normandy campaign became mobile. To save the German forces in Normandy from being completely encircled and destroyed a series of rapid withdrawals were undertaken through the Falaise-Argentan gap. On 16 August German forces continued retreating and crossed the River Orne. The *Hitlerjugend* division desperately fought to keep the gap open. The bulk of the German armour, however, that had become trapped inside the pocket at Falaise fought a desperate battle to escape the impending slaughter. By 21 August, the terrible fighting in what became famously known as the battle of the 'Falaise Pocket' drew to a catastrophic conclusion. The *Waffen-SS* had been dealt a heavy blow. (*IWM/Bundesarchive/M. Kaludow*)

Waffen-SS troops take cover from the systematic Allied bombing in the summer of 1944. The Normandy campaign had been very costly for the *Waffen-SS*, with many of its elite units being annihilated. Those elements that managed to escape the slaughter were withdrawn and refitted.

Reich Minister Joseph Goebbels poses for the camera with Artur Axmann with a newly decorated member of the *Hitlerjugend* in October 1942. Axmann was commander of the *Hitlerjugend* and during the last weeks of the war commanded units of the *Hitlerjugend* which had been incorporated into the *Volkssturm*. His units consisted mostly of children and adolescents. *(Roger Bender)*

Smiling for the camera, an *SS* motorcyclist during operations in 1943. It was not until October 1943 that the *SS Hitlerjugend* was officially designated as the *12.SS-Panzer-Division Hitlerjugend*. It was by far the youngest force in the *SS* arsenal with the average age around 17 years old.

During operations in northern France an unidentified *Hitlerjugend* unit on the march to its forward positions. It was here in France that these young boys fought fanatically against the Allied advance.

SS troops during fighting in northern France. These soldiers have taken cover and were armed with their distinctive Mauser rifles, which was the standard infantry weapon used by both the Wehrmacht and the *Waffen-SS*. Although very accurate, the Mauser had a very awkward and clumsy bolt action and only a five-round magazine, making rapid fire impossible.

An *SS Hitlerjugend* recruit armed with an MG34 machine gun in a light role on a bipod mounting. With many of the recruits so young commanders replaced the usual cigarette ration with sweets instead until the boys were old enough. (*HITM courtesy of Michael Cremin*)

An *SS* MG34 machine gunner accompanied by his squad during operations in France. These men are taking cover. Note the soldier with the camouflaged optical view finder, or Donkey's ears, as it was commonly nicknamed. (*HITM courtesy of Michael Cremin*)

A Panther with its commander surveying the terrain ahead in northern France in the summer of 1944. The total armoured strength of the *12.SS-Panzer-Division Hitlerjugend* comprised no less than 81 Panthers and 104 Pz.Kpfw.IVs. This was a very impressive array of armour. (*HITM courtesy of Michael Cremin*)

Chapter Four

Final Battles of the Reich

The military situation on the Eastern Front during the last six months of the war had become increasingly desperate for the Germans. Whilst many areas of the front simply cracked under the sheer weight of the Russian onslaught, a number of German units still continued to demonstrate their ability to defend the most hazardous positions against well-prepared and highly superior enemy forces. German infantry divisions bitterly contested large areas of the countryside. Fighting was often savage resulting in terrible casualties on both sides. Signs of disintegration now plagued every sector of the front. Almost continuously Soviet pressure was maintained, whilst German commanders strove desperately to stabilize the situation. Whilst some areas still held fanatically a general breakdown began to sweep the lines. German soldiers were completely stunned by the weight of the blow that had hit Army Group Centre. After more than ten days' fighting the battlefield had become wrought with death and destruction. Although the German soldier was generally determined as ever to fight, they were constantly being isolated and trapped by superior numbers of enemy infantry. Areas that still remained in German hands were slowly reduced to a few shrinking pockets of resistance.

As the situation deteriorated further the German High Command could do little to avert the looming catastrophe. The concern now was the severe lack of troops and equipment needed to hold new lines of defence. Because the Red Army had torn open the front lines, they had nothing in which to slow down the advance.

By the third week of January 1945 the military situation for the Germans became much worse as the Red Army launched a massive winter offensive. The principal objective was to crush the remaining German forces in Poland, East Prussia and the Baltic states. Along the Baltic an all-out Russian assault had begun in earnest to crush the remaining under-strength German units that had once formed *Heeresgruppe Nord*.

Here along the Baltic the German defenders attempted to stall the massive Russian push with the remaining weapons and men they had at their disposal. Every German soldier defending the area was aware of the significance if it was captured.

As the Reich became seriously threatened by a Russian invasion *Volkssturm*, *Hitlerjugend* together with civilians were drafted in to build defensive positions. Fox holes were dug in at intervals along roads and slit trenches for protection against low-flying aircraft were dug at considerable speed. Every hamlet, every isolated farmhouse, was linked by line or by a runner with a nearby town. The areas leading west towards the frontier of the Reich were defended by a mixed number of local militia, postal defence units, locally raised anti-tank groups, *Waffen-SS*, *Hitlerjugend*, and units of the *Volkssturm*. But in spite of the foreboding of what lay ahead, in the rank and file of the *Hitlerjugend*, morale still remained high. For these lads needed no propaganda to urge them on. They knew they were fighting to defend their homes and loved ones. All that was left for them was their skill and courage to get them through. Everything else, guns, planes and tanks had been sacrificed to impede the remorseless advance of the Allies and Russian forces.

As Russian tanks squealed and rattled remorselessly towards the first stretch of land that was Hitler's cherished Reich, units of the *Hitlerjugend* braced themselves before the fury of the Red Army. Along the borders of East Prussia Hitler's boy soldiers were quickly driven from their meagre defensive positions and pulverized into the rubble. When some determined units refused to budge, the Russians ordered in their flame-throwers to burn them out. Any *Hitlerjugend* or *Volkssturm* men that surrendered were normally regarded as partisans and simply herded together like cattle and executed. Over the next few days the battle for East Prussia went from bad to worse. Along the German front lines remnants of the *Heer*, *Waffen-SS*, *Volkssturm* and *Hitlerjugend* including thousands of civilians, fled the provinces of East Prussia under the savage advance of the Red Army. Although there were a number of *Volkssturm* and *Hitlerjugend* deserting their posts at the first available opportunity and changing into civilian dress, there were many more that were still determined as ever to fight a grim defence in front of the Russian onslaught. In southwest Poland situated on the River Oder the strategic town of Breslau had been turned into a fortress and defended by various *Volkssturm*, *Hitlerjugend*, *Waffen-SS* and various formations from the 269.*Infantry-Division*. During mid-February 1945 the German units put up a staunch defence with every available weapon that they could muster. As the battle raged, both German soldiers and civilians were cut to pieces by Russian attacks. During these vicious battles, which lasted until May 1945, there were many acts of courageous fighting. Cheering and yelling, old men and boys of the *Volkssturm* and *Hitlerjugend*, supported by ad hoc *SS* units, advanced across open terrain, sacrificing themselves in front of well-positioned Russian machine gunners and snipers. By the first week of March, Russian infantry had driven back the defenders into the inner city and were pulverizing it street by street. Lightly clad *SS*, *Volkssturm* and *Hitlerjugend* were still seen resisting, forced to fight in the sewers beneath the decimated city. When defenders of Breslau finally capitulated almost 60,000 Russian soldiers had been killed or wounded trying to capture the town, with some 29,000 German military and civilian casualties.

Elsewhere on the Eastern Front, fighting was merciless, with both sides imposing harsh measures on their men to stand where they were and fight to the death. In the *Heer* and *Waffen-SS* divisions, all malingerers were hanged by the roadside without even a summary court martial. Those who deserted or caused self-inflicted wounds were executed on the spot. Soldiers would regularly pass groups of freshly erected gallows, where the *SS* and *Feldgendarmerie* had hanged 'deserters'.

With every defeat and withdrawal came ever-increasing pressure on the commanders to exert harsher discipline on their weary men. The thought of fighting on German soil for the first time resulted in mixed feelings among the soldiers. Although the defence of the Reich automatically stirred emotional feelings to fight for their land, not all soldiers felt the same way. More and more young conscripts were showing signs that they did not want to die for a lost cause. Conditions on the Eastern Front were miserable not only for the newest recruits, but also for battle-hardened soldiers who had survived many months of bitter conflict against the Red Army.

Within weeks of the Russian drive east, the Soviets had reached the River Oder and by mid-April had attacked from this important river line and burst open onto the road to Berlin. Those *Waffen-SS* troops that had not been decimated including the last remnants of the *Hitlerjugend* were to take part in the last, apocalyptic struggle to save the Reich capital from the clutches of the Red Army. In spite of the fervent attempts by these young warriors of the Führer's elite, by 25 April Berlin was completely surrounded, and the next day around 500,000 Soviet troops bulldozed their way through the city.

Hitler's reinforcements now consisted of fewer than 5,000 *Luftwaffe* personnel and *Hitlerjugend*, all armed with hand-held weapons. The city was doomed. For the next week the battle for Berlin raged. Yet, in spite of the dire situation members of the *Hitlerjugend, Volkssturm, Luftwaffe* and *Heer* were ordered to fight to the death and anyone found deserting or shirking from their duties was hunted down by *Reichsführer* Heinrich Himmler's personal Escort battalion and hanged from the nearest lamppost. But even in the last days of the war the *SS* proved an efficient, formidable and ruthless fighting machine.

Berlin was almost defenceless against the mighty Red Army. The *Volkssturm* was given the main task of defending the city which was supported by a motley collection of *Hitlerjugend*. However, supplies were desperately low. There were no less than fifteen different types of rifles and ten kinds of machine-guns, many of which had been salvaged from a number of occupied countries. The average ammunition supply was about five rounds per rifle. Many of these German units which were aged between ten and sixty years old were expected to defend their positions with these guns against well equipped enemy troops which were often supported by the Soviet Army's formidable tanks and SP guns. Those that were fortunate enough to be armed with the *Panzerfaust* stood more of a chance. Thus, when the Russians finally bulldozed their way through Berlin, they flamed, bombarded and machine-gunned the defenders, crushing them into the piles of rubble that littered the city. Where *Hitlerjugend* and other supported units managed to desperately put up a determined resistance the whole area was saturated with Katyusha rocket fire, and then the tanks would go in to destroy the dazed survivors with machine-gun fire and high explosives. Many of the captured and wounded were executed on the spot and left suspended from the lamp posts as a warning to others if they resisted.

In some areas, however, the *Hitlerjugend* managed to knock out a number of Russian tanks with their *Panzerfäuste*, but even these courageous fighters were no match to the hardened soldiers that had fought their way bitterly from Stalingrad two years earlier. Even so, the *Panzerfaust* had become a much respected weapon among Russian soldiers and tank crews. In fact, the *Hitlerjugend* in some areas of the city had become so successful one unit was actually decorated on 20 March 1945 in the bombed and shelled Reich Chancellery gardens personally by Hitler.

Even as the last hours were fought out in the fiery cauldron of Berlin, *SS* units, lacking all provisions including many types of weapons, effectively halted and stemmed a number of Russian assaults.

By 1 May Berlin was captured, and although the war was more or less over numerous groupings of undestroyed *Hitlerjugend* bands went into hiding and began a series of guerrilla actions. In a number of areas of Germany and Austria, there were half-demoralized radicals attempting to resist. The Nazi youths were told to continue to resist and ambush Allied troops, to string decapitation wires, lay mines and booby-trap roads. To help to continue their resistance, thousands of *Hitlerjugend* were ordered to flee to the mountains. Although it is unknown how many of these youths actually reached the southern mountains of Bavaria, the area did erupt in active partisan warfare. In the relative safety of the Austrian mountains, *Hitlerjugend* units terrorized collaborators and laid mines. Small units were also fielded in the western Alps, where they were armed from old *Waffen-SS* stocks. Here in these winding mountains, fanatical youths played children being dead in the roadways as American infantrymen approached, only to pick themselves up once the Americans had passed, and then open fire on them from the rear.

For the next six months in these mountains there was still spot resistance and determined efforts by their commanders to keep fighting, the continual teachings of National Socialism, when hope was so clearly lost, was one demand too many upon the spirit of the youths. The fervent attempt to unify and organize an entire generation of children for warfare had finally failed.

During winter operations on the Eastern Front in late 1944. Here *Hitlerjugend* and their *Heer* counterparts in a flak position somewhere on the Baltic Front. The FlaK gun is a 20mm quadruple self-propelled FlaK 38. The weapon could engage not only air targets but ground ones as well. With the folding sides down the gun was very adaptable and could traverse 360 degrees, making it a deadly weapon of war. (*HITM courtesy of Michael Cremin*)

A group of SS and young *Heer* troops during operations on the Eastern Front in the winter of 1944. These troops have dug a trench position inside a forest. Everywhere along the bombed and blasted front lines the Germans were being constantly forced to retreat. Many isolated units often comprising a motley collection of *Heer*, *Volkssturm*, *Hitlerjugend* and *Waffen-SS* troops spent hours or even days fighting a bloody defence. Russian soldiers frequently requested them to surrender and assured them that no harm would come to them if they did so. But despite this reassuring tone, most German troops continued to fight to the bitter end. To the German soldier in 1945 they were fighting an enemy that they not only despised, but also were terrified of. (*HITM courtesy of Michael Cremin*)

Wehrmacht and *Hitlerjugend* forces somewhere on the Eastern Front during the late winter of 1944. A feeling of despair and gloom now gripped the German front lines. Among the soldiers there was a dull conviction that the war was lost, and yet there was still no sight of its end. Being always outnumbered, perpetually short of fuel and ammunition, and having to constantly exert themselves and their machinery to the very limits of endurance had a profound effect on life at the front. The vehicle is a Sd.Kfz.11 3-tonne halftrack prime mover. (*HITM courtesy of Michael Cremin*)

A soldier on the front line with an MG34 machine gun on a sustained fire mount. The effect of starving parts of the front line that required reinforcements to contain the enemy was a constant concern for the tacticians. Many soldiers including the elite divisions of the *Waffen-SS* did receive a high proportion of tanks, artillery and assault guns, but this was in stark contrast to the enormous volume of armaments being produced by the Russians. German forces were thus faced with a dangerous and worsening prospect, and were compelled to use *Hitlerjugend* and *Volkssturm* soldiers to help bolster the dwindling front lines on both the Eastern and Western front. Surprisingly, many of these troops, in particular the *Hitlerjugend* still proved to be formidable opponents against the growing Soviet 'menace'.

Troops preparing their *Nebelwerfer* for a fire mission. The weapon was known as the NbW41, which was a six-barrelled rocket launcher mounted on a two-wheeled carriage. The rockets were fired one at a time, in a timed ripple, but the launcher had no capability to fire single rockets. (*HITM courtesy of Michael Cremin*)

Two photographs showing the rockets belonging to the 150mm *Nebelwerfer* 41. Note the troops manhandling the 2.5kg shells from the specially designed cradle on its trailer. When fired the projectiles could be projected over a range of 7,000 metres screaming through the air, causing the enemy to become unnerved by the noise. These fearsome weapons caused extensive carnage on enemy lines. They often served in independent army rocket launcher battalions, and later in the war in regiments and brigades. *(M. Kaludow)*

A young soldier manning a trench with his Mauser rifle at the ready. These youngsters were fearless to the last. Often with little training they were put along the front lines to defend their meagre positions with a mixture of *Waffen-SS*, *Heer* and *Volkssturm* troops. Many were quickly wiped out as a result.

A photograph showing two *Hitlerjugend* troops armed with the lethal *Panzerschreck* or tank terror. The popular name given by the troops to this weapon was the *Raketenpanzerbüchse* (rocket tank rifle), abbreviated to RPzB. It was an 88mm reusable anti-tank rocket launcher developed during the latter half of the war. Another popular nickname was *Ofenrohr* or stove pipe.

A young *Waffen-SS* soldier with an MG34 machine gun slung over his shoulder for ease of carriage. Rifle groups generally had a light machine-gun with a bipod, along with one or two spare barrels. A heavy machine-gun group, however, had the bipod fitted machine gun, but additionally carried a tripod with optical sight.

A youthful *Luftwaffe* FlaK gunner with his 20mm FlaK 30 crew preparing for a fire mission against an enemy target. The projectiles used by this weapon were airburst shells. The airburst shells were favoured for their anti-personnel capabilities against troops in cover. The explosive force of a 20mm HE shell was small, about the same as a hand grenade.

Two young *Waffen-SS* heavy machine gunners well concealed behind foliage inside what appears to be a bomb crater. This machine gun is on a sustained fire mount. In open terrain the MG34 machine gun squad would use their sustained fire mount to protect the flanks of advancing rifle companies. However, in built-up areas the crews often had to operate forward with the rifle platoons and in light machine gun roles with bipods only. They were able to still sometimes take advantage of the situation and revert back to a heavy machine gun role.

A young group of *Waffen-SS* FlaK gunners with their 20mm quadruple self-propelled FlaK 38 gun during operations in 1944. This weapon has been mounted on the back of a truck with appliqué armour added to the cab. The FlaK gun could engage not only air targets but ground ones as well. With the folding sides down the gun was very adaptable and could traverse 360 degrees, making it a very formidable weapon of war.

Heer and *Hitlerjugend* troops man a 20mm FlaK 38 defensive position probably during the defence of the Reich in early 1945. Aerial attacks across the German front were merciless and often unceasing. The Soviet Air Force caused unprecedented amounts of destruction to German defensive positions from which many could not recover. (*HITM courtesy of Michael Cremin*)

Recruited *SS* troops withdrawing to another defensive position during operations in 1944. Both soldiers are armed with the excellent 7.9mm Kar98k carbine, a compact and reliable bolt-action Mauser design which was widely used in both the *Heer* and *Waffen-SS*. By this period of the war the *Waffen-SS* were regularly being used as a special 'fire brigade' force. During these defensive operations the *Waffen-SS* often supported by a 'mixed bag' of *Hitlerjugend* and *Volkssturm* were ordered to try to plug gaps in the front wherever they appeared. But the German military situation in late 1944 had been a complete disaster in the East. Although in a number of areas the Soviet advance had been stemmed by fanatical German resistance, it was only a matter of time before defeat became inevitable.

A Sd.Kfz.10 1-tonne halftrack can be seen towing a stricken support vehicle that has evidently broken down in a freezing river. Whilst the Germans had conditioned themselves for the arctic conditions of the Soviet Union, movement was constantly hindered by the ice and snow.

A mixture of young and old *Heer* troops during the late winter 1944/45 moving in columns along an icy road somewhere in the East. The average age of a German soldier recruited during this period of the war was seventeen years old. But in spite of the foreboding of what lay ahead, in the rank and file of the young that went to battle, morale still remained high. For these lads needed no propaganda to urge them on. They knew they were fighting to defend their homes and loved ones. All that was left for them was their skill and courage to get them through.

Out in the field moving along a road are two *Jagdpanzer* IV. The *Jagdpanzer* IV was an effective tank destroyer, but by the time it left the factory its unique defensive attributes mattered little any more. Following this formidable machine are grenadiers armed with the deadly *Panzerfaust*. (*HITM courtesy of Michael Cremin*)

A column of Sd.Kfz.250 and Sd.Kfz.251 Ausf.C halftracks with *Waffen-SS* troops riding onboard. In the background on the right is a Pz.Kpfw.III, fitted with track extensions to cope with the muddy conditions. This photograph was most probably taken during the latter period of the war in western Poland in late 1944.

A 37mm FlaK 36 gun in a defensive position being operated by a young crew. These deadly guns were much respected by low-flying Russian airmen and were also particularly devastating against light vehicles, as well as troops caught in the open. The weapon also armed a variety of vehicles on self-propelled mounts where they could be moved from one part of the defensive line to another quickly and efficiently.

Three photographs showing Russian artillery in action against German positions in early 1945. Due to a serious lack of troop reserves many parts of the German front were now defended by a mixed number of local militia, postal defence units, locally raised anti-tank groups, *Heer*, *Waffen-SS* and *Allegemein-SS* formations, *Hitlerjugend*, and units of the *Volkssturm*. But surprisingly, even in the rank and file of the *Volkssturm*, morale remained high. Along the frontier of the Reich the German defensive lines were soon turned into a wall of flame and smoke as the Russians launched their attacks. For the *Volkssturm* and *Hitlerjugend*, many were going into action for the first time, and a number of them felt excited at the thought of fighting an offensive that their *Führer* had said would drive the invaders from their homeland and win new victories in the East. But this conflict was fought without rules, and new conscripts soon discovered the terrors of fighting superior Russian soldiers. The photographs show Soviet 122mm M-30 howitzers in action.

Heer, *Volkssturm*, and *Hitlerjugend* recruits are given a quick lesson in the use of the *Panzerfaust*. By 1945 there was a dramatic increase in the loss of Russian tanks to the *Panzerfaust* and more than half of the tanks knocked out in combat were destroyed by either *Panzerfaust* or *Panzerschreck*.

A *Hitlerjugend* grenadier moves through a wooded area armed with the deadly *Panzerfaust*. The *Panzerfaust* literally meant armour or tank fist. This disposable anti-tank weapon was in mass production in late 1944 and scored sizable successes against enemy tanks. To the *SS* volunteer soldier facing the might of the enemy, the outcome was almost certain death. The realization among the German soldiers that they might be fighting a losing battle was seldom admitted openly. Most of them already knew that the end would come soon. They were not convinced by their commanders' encouragements especially when they were lying in their trenches subjected to hours of bombardments by guns that never seemed to lack shells. Out on the battlefield *Heer*, *Waffen-SS*, *Volkssturm* and *Hitlerjugend* forces were urged on, not to fight and do their duty for the *Führer*, but to defend their land against the advancing Red Army.

Smiling *Hitlerjugend* troops pictured here attached to an unidentified *Wehrmacht* unit. Along the front line to the east of Berlin the defences were made up of *Hitlerjugend* and *Volkssturm* forces supported by a mixture of *Heer, Waffen-SS* and Panzer troops. But even these courageous fighters were no match for hardened soldiers that had fought their way bitterly through Russia to the gates of the Reich.

Troops during the last weeks of the war trudge along a road with a captured Soviet Maxim 1910 machine gun.

Two soldiers in one of the many defensive shelter positions erected along the German front during the last months of the war. These shelters were called *Halbgruppenunterstand* (group and half-group living bunkers). These were to become essential for both *Heer* and *Waffen-SS* troops if they were to survive the ceaseless artillery and terrible freezing weather conditions.

Heer and *Hitlerjugend* prisoners of war shuffle along a dirt road into captivity in early 1945. By this period of the war signs of disintegration plagued every sector of the front. Almost continuous Soviet and Allied pressure was maintained, whilst German commanders strove desperately to stabilise the situation. Whilst some areas still held fanatically a general breakdown began to sweep the lines. *(M. Kaludow)*

A mix of dejected *Waffen-SS* troops, some comprising the famous *12.SS.Panzer-Division Hitlerjugend* being sent to the rear as POWs. (National Archives)

Both young and old conscripts are seen here after being rounded up and taken away as prisoners of war. Although the war was more or less over numerous groupings of un-destroyed *Hitlerjugend* bands went into hiding and began a series of guerrilla actions. In a number of areas of Germany and Austria, there were half-demoralized radicals attempting to resist. The Nazi youths were told to continue to resist and ambush Allied troops, to string decapitation wires, lay mines and booby-trap roads. To help to continue their resistance, thousands of *Hitlerjugend* were ordered to flee to the mountains. (IWM/M. Kaludow)

A young lad conscripted into the *Heer* to help support the dwindling forces on both the Western and Eastern Fronts is photographed as a prisoner of war. (*Roger Bender*)

US troops are seen here with a captured youth of the 12.*SS.Panzer-Division Hitlerjugend* in April 1945. (*National Archives*)

US soldiers pose for the camera parading two captured young *Waffen-SS* soldiers in April 1945. (*National Archives*)

A blood soaked captured young soldier of the 12.*SS.Panzer-Division Hitlerjugend* moves toward British lines during operations in April 1945. (*IWM/National Archives*)

This photograph shows Soviet troops in action against German units that are fanatically defending their positions to the last. As the Reich became seriously threatened by a Russian invasion *Volkssturm* and *Hitlerjugend* troops, together with civilians, were drafted in to build defensive positions. Fox holes were dug-in at intervals along roads and slit trenches for protection against low-flying aircraft were dug at considerable speed. Every hamlet, every isolated farmhouse, was linked by line or by a runner with a nearby town. The areas leading west towards the frontier of the Reich were defended by a mixed number of local militia, postal defence units, locally raised anti-tank groups, *Waffen-SS*, *Hitlerjugend*, and units of the *Volkssturm*. But in spite of the foreboding of what lay ahead, in the rank and file of the *Hitlerjugend*, morale still remained high. (*M. Kaludow*)

Two captured *Hitlerjugend* soldiers pose for the camera following their capture in April 1945. These youngsters were almost defenceless against both the Red Army and Allies. The *Volkssturm* was given the main task of defending key areas which was supported by a motley collection of *Hitlerjugend*. However, supplies were desperately low. *(Roger Bender)*

The smiles of these three young *Hitlerjugend* recruits say it all — relieved to be captured. This photograph was taken by US troops, probably in April 1945. *(National Archives)*

A captured youngster of the *Hitlerjugend* photographed by his American captors in April 1945. (*Roger Bender*)

A smiling young *Hitlerjugend* recruit poses for the camera following his capture by US troops in April 1945.
(*National Archives*)

Appendix One

12.SS-Panzer-Division 'Hitlerjugend'

Order of Battle: France, June 1944

Brigadeführer Fritz Witt (killed in action 14 June 1944)
Oberführer Kurt Meyer (from 14 June 1944)
Sturmbannführer Hubert Meyer (from 6 September 1944)
Brigadeführer Fritz Kraemer (from 24 October 1944)
Brigadeführer Hugo Kraas (from 13 November 1944 – 8 May 1945)

25th SS Panzergrenadier Regiment Hitlerjugend (*Standartenführer* Kurt Meyer
(until 14 June 1944), *Obersturmbannführer* Karl-Heinz Milius (from 14 June 1944)
I. Battalion (*Sturmbannführer* Hans Waldmüller (killed in action 8 September 1944))
1st Company
2nd Company
3rd Company
4th (Heavy) Company
II. Battalion
III. Battalion (*Obersturmbannführer* Karl-Heinz Milius (until 14 June 1944),
Obersturmbannführer Fritz Steiger (from 14 June 1944))
13th (Panzerabwehrkanone) Company
14th Company
15th Aufklärung (Reconnaissance) Company
16th (Pionier) Company

26th SS Panzergrenadier Regiment Hitlerjugend
(*Standartenführer* Wilhelm Mohnke)
I. Battalion, Sturmbannführer Bernhard Krause
1st Company

2nd Company
3rd Company
4th (Heavy) Company
II. Battalion, Sturmbannführer Bernhard Siebken
III. Battalion, Sturmbannführer Erich Olboeter

13th (Panzerabwehrkanone) Company (*Obersturmführer* Polanski)
14th Company
15th Reconnaissance Company
16th (Pionier) Company

12th SS Panzer Regiment (*Obersturmbannführer* Max Wünsche)
I. Battalion Sturmbannführer Arnold Jürgensen
1st Company
2nd Company
3rd Company
4th Company
Repair Company

II. Battalion (*Sturmbannführer* Karl-Heinz Prinz)
5th Company
6th Company
7th Company
8th Company
9th Company
Repair Company

12th SS Artillery Regiment (*Sturmbannführer* Fritz Schröder)
I. Battalion
II. Battalion
III. Battalion
12th SS Motorrad (Motorcycle) Regiment

12th SS Reconnaissance Battalion (*Sturmbannführer* Gerhard Bremer)
1st Company
2nd Company
3rd Company
4th Company
5th (Heavy) Company

12th SS Panzerjäger Battalion (*Sturmbannführer* Jacob Hanreich)
1st Battery
2nd Battery

12th SS Werfer Battalion (*Hauptsturmführer* Willy Müller)
I Battery
II Battery
III Battery

12th SS FlaK Battalion (*Hauptsturmführer* Rudolf Fend)
I Battery
II Battery
III Battery
IV Battery

12th SS Pionier (Pioneer) Battalion (*Sturmbannführer* Siegfried Müller)
1st Company
2nd Company
3rd Company
Motorized Bridging Unit

12th SS Panzer Nachrichten (Signals) Battalion
12th SS Instandsetzungs
12th SS Nachschub Truppen
12th SS Wirtschafts Battalion
12th SS Kriegsberichter (War Reporter) platoon (mot)
12th SS Sanitäts (Medical) Battalion
12th SS Fuhrerbewerber Lehrgange
12th SS Feldgendarmerie Company
12th SS Feldpost (Field Post) office

Appendix Two

12th Army, April 1945

In April 1945 the 12th Army was placed into defensive positions along the Elbe River facing west. But, in response to approaching Soviet forces from the east, the army was re-positioned to face that threat. During the last days of April the army failed to relieve Hitler in the besieged capital city during the Battle of Berlin. It was in the 12th Army that the *Hitlerjugend* fought a number of successful engagements in a tank destroying brigade.

General Walter Wenck

XX Corps (Gen Carl-Erik Koehler)
   'Theodor Körner' RAD Division
   'Ulrich von Hutten' Infantry Division
   'Ferdinand von Schill' Infantry Division
   'Scharnhorst' Infantry Division

General Karl Arndt

XXXIX Panzer Corps
(12–21 April 1945 under OKW with the following structure)
   'Clausewitz' Panzer Division
   'Schlageter' RAD Division
   84th Infantry Division
(21–26 April 1945 under 12th Army with the following structure)
   'Clausewitz' Panzer Division
   84th Infantry Division
   'Hamburg' Reserve Infantry Division
   'Meyer' Infantry Division
XXXXI Panzer Corps (Lt Gen Holste)
   'von Hake' Infantry Division
   199th Infantry Division 'V-Weapons' Infantry Division
   1st Hitlerjugend (HJ) Tank Destroyer Bde
   'Hermann Göring' Jagdpanzer Bde

General Maximillian Reichsherr von Edelscheim

XXXXVIII Panzer Corps
  14th FlaK Division
  'Leipzig' Battle Group
  'Halle' Battle Group

Notes